09 2014

WITHDRAWN

Mysterious Monsters

Searching FOR EL CHUPACABRA

Jennifer Rivkin

PowerKiDS
press

New York

Published in 2015 by The Rosen Publishing Group, Inc.
29 East 21st Street, New York, NY 10010

Produced for Rosen by BlueApple*Works* Inc.
Art Director: Tibor Choleva
Designer: Joshua Avramson
Photo Research: Jane Reid
Editor for BlueApple*Works*: Melissa McClellan
US Editor: Joshua Shadowens

Illustrations: Cover Kresimir Kirasic; p. 4-5 Valentina Photos/Shutterstock; p. 6 top hektor2/Shutterstock; p. 6 left, 26 right, 27 Atula Siriwardane; p. 6 right, 7 top John Bright; p. 8 ekler/Shutterstock; p. 10 top Victor Habbick; p. 12 Carlyn Iverson; p. 14 right,15, 18 top, 18 bottom, 20, 28 T. Choleva; p. 26 top left Bob Orsillo/Shutterstock; p. 28 front breaker213/Shutterstock

Photo Credits: Cover background artshock/Shutterstock; p. 1 background Francey; p. 1 breaker213/Shutterstock; p. 6 background Kiev.Victor/Shutterstock; p. 7 right leoks/Shutterstock; p. 8 top Robert Crum/Dreamstime; p. 9 basel101658/Shutterstock; p. 10 CreativeNature.nl/Shutterstock; p. 10 bottom Orientaly/Shutterstock; p 11 Benjamin Radford; p. 12-13 background BMJ/Shutterstock; p. 12 top Jan-Dirk Hansen/Shutterstock; p. 13 John Panella/Shutterstock; p 14-15 background ARENA Creative/Shutterstock; p 14 top Ruth Peterkin/Shutterstock; p. 14 jo Crebbin/Shutterstock; p. 15 front Goodluz /Shutterstock; p. 16-17 background Mircea Bezergheanu /Shutterstock; p. 16 top WitthayaP/Shutterstock; p. 16 top right Bob Orsillo/Shutterstock; p. 16 bottom left Kirsanov Valeriy Vladimirovich/Shutterstock; p. 17 Jonathan Downes; p. 18-19 background Triff/Shutterstock; p. 19 right Ralf Juergen Kraft/Shutterstock; p. 19 far right Bruce Rolff/Shutterstock; p. 20 top Julien_N/Shutterstock; p. 20 front Goodluz/ Shutterstock; p. 21 rthoma/Shutterstock; p 22 top Chris Hill/Shutterstock; p. 22 left Mikelane45/Dreamstime; p. 22 right Markuso/Shutterstock; p. 23 Kozoriz Yuriy/Shutterstock; p. 24-25 background Georg Schmidt/Shutterstock; p. 24 top Monkey Business Images/Shutterstock; p. 24 middle Suphatthra China/Shutterstock; p.25 right Eugene Chernetsov/Shutterstock; p. 26 top andreiuc88/Shutterstock; p. 26 background Feraru Nicolae/Shutterstock; p. 26 background Feraru Nicolae/Shutterstock; p. 27 background Krivosheev Vitaly/Shutterstock

Library of Congress Cataloging-in-Publication-Data

Rivkin, Jennifer, author.
Searching for el Chupacabra / by Jennifer Rivkin.
    pages cm. — (Mysterious monsters)
Includes index.
ISBN 978-1-4777-7113-6 (library binding) — ISBN 978-1-4777-7114-3 (pbk.) —
ISBN 978-1-4777-7115-0 (6-pack)
1. Chupacabras—Juvenile literature. I. Title.
QL89.2.C57R58 2015
001.944—dc22
                            2014004878

Manufactured in the United States of America

CPSIA Compliance Information: Batch #WS14PK8 For Further Information contact: Rosen Publishing, New York, New York at 1-800-237-9932

TABLE OF CONTENTS

What Is a Chupacabra?

Everyone is scared of something that makes their heart beat faster and the hairs stand up on the back of their neck. For little children, monsters under the bed are a common source of nightmares. Parents assure them over and over again that there is no such thing as monsters. But are grownups right? Not everyone thinks so. Some people believe that creatures called el Chupacabra are real flesh-and-blood beasts that are roaming the Earth right now, just waiting to prey on the innocent.

What if it's true? Maybe el Chupacabras (or Chupacabra) is just a myth. But if it's true…let's just say that it's a good idea to learn as much as you can about the creature. Read on for everything that you need to know about el Chupacabras.

EYEWITNESS TALE

In 1996, Luis Guadalupe, of Puerto Rico, said he came too close to a Chupacabra. Guadalupe explained that he saw the demon-like beast flying through the air. The creature, which was able to change colors, had a long, pointy tongue and looked like it was out for blood. Guadalupe fled for his life. Wouldn't you?

EL CHUPACABRA EXPLAINED

Chupacabra comes from the Spanish words *chupar* "to suck" and *cabra* "goat." The name literally translates to "goat sucker." This is because, as legend has it, the Chupacabra drains the blood from its victims (usually livestock, such as goats and chickens). Predators like coyotes eat the meat of their prey, resulting in a **carcass** that's picked apart. The Chupacabra leaves behind only round **puncture** marks in the victim's neck. Those who believe in el Chupacabra think it is responsible for hundreds of animal deaths over the years.

WHAT CHUPACABRA LOOKS LIKE

The most important thing to know when preparing for the possibility of an encounter with a monster is what to look for. The fact that no one is clear about the Chupacabra's appearance makes the creature that much more terrifying. One thing that all descriptions have in common is the Chupacabra's razor-sharp fangs. Yikes!

Chupacabra as a Kangaroo:
Some eyewitnesses describe Chupacabra as having legs like a kangaroo and the head of a dog. They say the creature jumps or hops.

Chupacabra as a Reptile:
Others say the creature is lizard-like with a forked tongue, scaly, greenish-gray skin, and long spines down the center of its back.

DIFFERING DESCRIPTIONS

Chupacabra as a Dog:
A third description of the creature says that it looks like a hairless dog, with a ridge down its back and front legs shorter than the rear. Sometimes the animal is described as having long quills, or spines, that follow the ridge of its back.

Chupacabra as a Demon:
Many eyewitnesses have described Chupacabra as having glowing red or yellow eyes. Several have said that it has wings, flies, and looks like a gargoyle.

▶ *A gargoyle is a grotesquely carved human or animal figure that can sometimes be seen on old buildings. Gargoyles are said to frighten off and protect what they guard, such as a building or a church, from any harmful and evil spirits.*

WHERE CHUPACABRA PROWLS

Most Chupacabra sightings have taken place in the Americas. Puerto Rico, Chile, and Mexico are prime hunting grounds for the creature. It has also been spotted across the United States, from Florida to Oregon, especially in Spanish-speaking communities. But the Chupacabra (or at least the idea of it) has been continent-hopping recently. Reports have come in from countries that are oceans away from North America, including Russia, Portugal, China, and the Philippines.

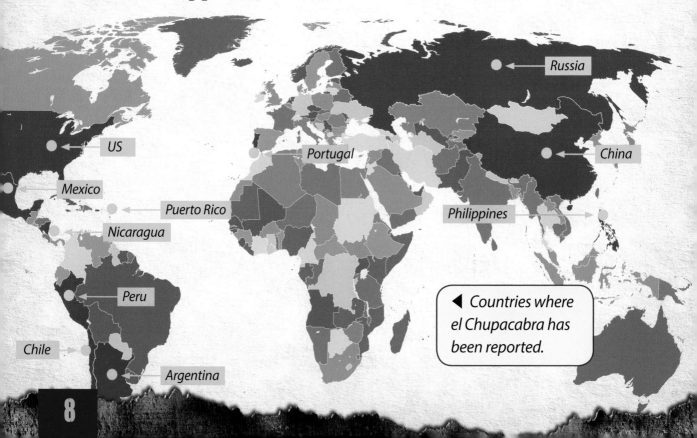

Russia

US

Portugal

China

Mexico

Puerto Rico

Philippines

Nicaragua

Peru

Chile

Argentina

◀ Countries where el Chupacabra has been reported.

Chupacabra Habitat

The Chupacabra must not be picky about the type of environment that it prefers. It has been seen—or has left evidence—in many locations. From the rainforest to the desert, the Chupacabra is on the hunt. The creature may go unnoticed deep in the jungle or woods, where an animal laying on the ground with a puncture wound in its neck would never be discovered by humans. Closer to civilization, the Chupacabra has been spotted near farms and ranches.

Did You Know?

The first Chupacabra sighting took place in Puerto Rico, an island in the Caribbean Sea. Puerto Rico is about 1,000 miles (1,600 km) southeast of Florida. The island was formed millions of years ago as a result of volcanic activity. For this reason, there are no large land mammals native to the island. The mammals that are now in Puerto Rico are there because humans brought them. For example, mongooses were introduced to control the population of mice and rats that came to the island on ships and in cargo. Livestock (like sheep and goats) were brought to the island for farming. This begs the question, if the Chupacabra is a mammal, when—and how—did it get to Puerto Rico?

▶ The monster seems to prefer farms near forested areas for easy escape and that are close to a water source.

THE MYSTERY BEGINS

Many famous monster sightings date back thousands of years. For example, the first observation of Scotland's Loch Ness monster was recorded in the sixth century. Chupacabra is a relatively new in the long history of monsters. The first eyewitness came forward in the 1990s.

In 1995, over 100 farm animals were found dead in Puerto Rico. The deaths caused a panic among the citizens of the island, especially because all of the animals had unexplained puncture wounds in their necks. Something strange was going on.

◀ *All the animals killed by Chupacabra are described as having big round puncture marks on their bodies.*

THE TOLENTINO STORY

The mystery became even more bizarre after Madelyne Tolentino came forward with her story. She told a newspaper reporter that she saw a creature standing upright on two legs, with body hair dotted with patches of skin, large eyes, curved clawed fingers and toes, quills down its back, and fangs. She said that the creature jumped like a kangaroo. Many people believed that the riddle had been solved. This beast was responsible for the slaughter.

▶ Benjamin Radford, an investigator and deputy editor of Skeptical Inquirer magazine, became suspicious of Tolentino's story when he realized that the creature she described was almost identical to the monster in the movie Species, which came out in 1995. Tolentino admitted to Radford that she had seen the film not long before she saw the "chupacabra." Could her imagination have played tricks on her? It's very possible.

NASTY BEHAVIOR

It can be disturbing to watch a nature documentary focused on a predator attacking its prey. A lion slowly and quietly stalks a gazelle, the chase is on, and the lion finally pounces, tearing the flesh from the now lifeless victim. Not a pretty picture.

The Chupacabra might just take alarming eating habits to a whole new level. Farmers have reported that their animals were not just eaten, but were horribly mutilated and had their blood drained. This happened to not just one animal, but to hundreds.

▶ Some witnesses say that the Chupacabra paralyzes its prey with its eyes so that it can suck the animal's blood while it is still alive.

INTELLIGENT MONSTER

The Chupacabra attacks animals that won't fight back, such as sheep, rabbits, and chickens. Perhaps the most troubling part of the Chupacabra story is the idea that it must be extremely intelligent to kill so many animals without being caught. Chicken coops can protect animals from creatures like coyotes, but they are apparently no match for a Chupacabra. Some farmers claim that the beast gets in and out, killing the chickens and leaving the coop undisturbed.

EYEWITNESS TALE

In 1996, Enrique Barreto, a farmer from Puerto Rico, discovered one of his sheep lying on the ground. It was dead from an apparent puncture wound to the neck. Police officers who came to investigate witnessed something even stranger—an orange-eyed creature, standing on two legs and staring at them as if stalking prey. Neighbors later claimed to see the same creature sitting in a tree and hissing. The sightings weren't exactly the same, but they had one thing in common. Anyone who looked into the creature's eyes said that they immediately felt faint.

◀ Chickens are often kept in a building called a chicken coop or hen house. The birds lay their eggs in nest boxes and sleep on perches inside the coop. The hen house protects chickens from bad weather and predators.

CHUPACABRAS IN PUERTO RICO

After the original animal killings in Puerto Rico, the government put Civil Defense officials in charge of investigating. The mayor of Canóvanas, Puerto Rico, José Soto, organized a hunt for the beast. Once a week for a year, using a caged goat as bait, volunteers set out to find the animal in the hills surrounding Canóvanas. The search didn't lead to any solid evidence, but Soto warned that the beast was "highly intelligent."

◀ Wild dogs do not have owners. They live on their own in rural areas and cities all over the world. Wild dogs eat whatever they can find. They often attack livestock since they are easier to catch than wild animals. They usually stay away from humans.

No Need to Panic?

When the Chupacabra story broke out in the 1990s, Puerto Rican government officials were quick to try and calm citizens down. They assured the people that although over 100 animals had been killed, there was no need to panic—there was no such thing as el Chupacabra. They said that the reports had been caused by overactive imaginations or **hoaxes**.

To prove it, they had veterinarians do **autopsies** on 20 animals that locals believed were killed by the Chupacabra. The vets believed that the animals with bite wounds were killed by wild dogs. They also found that the animals were not completely drained of blood. The amount of blood the animals had left was what could be expected from an animal that had bled because of a regular bite.

▶ The vets did autopsies on the animals. They found that the animals had died from parasites, bite wounds from wild dogs, and other causes.

CHUPACABRAS ELSEWHERE

The first Chupacabra reports came from Puerto Rico, but since then, sightings have been noted around the world. People have claimed to see the Chupacabra in Russia, Portugal, China, the Philippines, Peru, Argentina, Nicaragua, Chile, and Mexico.

In 2005, some farmers from Russian villages began losing animals to mysterious deaths. The animals' necks were punctured and their bodies left bloodless. Sound familiar? Eyewitnesses described a kangaroo-type creature as the **culprit**. One witness said that the animal jumped easily over the farm's fence. Another saw a pack of the predators, including "puppies."

▲ *Some villagers organized night patrols. Volunteers stayed up through the night to protect the animals and try to capture the creature.*

CHUPACABRAS IN THE US

There have been hundreds of reported Chupacabra sightings across the United States. Over several years leading up to 2007, Phylis Canion, who owned a ranch in Cuero, Texas, found her chickens—28 of them—dead and bloodless, with wounds in their throats. In 2007, she found the remains of a "blue-skinned" dog that could have been a Chupacabra. She believes this creature was responsible for the massacre.

EYEWITNESS TALE

In 2013, a family in Picayune, Mississippi saw what they believed to be a Chupacabra. They posted a video online. In an interview with reporters, eyewitness Jennifer Whitfield said: "If a zombie had a dog, that's what it would look like." While Whitfield and others may be convinced that they saw a mythical beast, representatives from the Mississippi Department of Wildlife, Fisheries, and Parks believe the animal to be a coyote with mange, a skin disease caused by mites.

◀ The animal Canion found had fangs and gray skin, three toes on its paws, and strange pouches on either side of its tail. DNA tests showed that the animal was a mix of coyote and Mexican wolf. However, Canion still believes that there was something different about it. Whether or not the "Blue Dog" was a Chupacabra, Canion's story got people interested in the creature again.

GOVERNMENT CONSPIRACY THEORY

Many **conspiracy theorists** believe that the government is trying to cover up the truth—that the Chupacabra exists.

In Chile, the newspapers have reported incredible stories about the creature. In 2000, after sheep and goats were killed in Calama, Chile, the National Guard was sent to investigate. Soldiers searched for the animal that was behind the killings. They reported that some of the creatures were caught and killed. Then, US government officials took the bodies away.

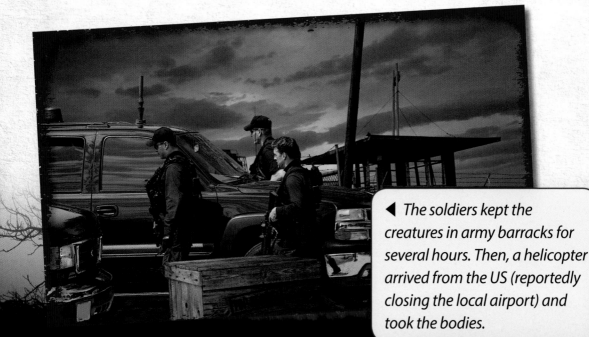

◀ *The soldiers kept the creatures in army barracks for several hours. Then, a helicopter arrived from the US (reportedly closing the local airport) and took the bodies.*

Why would the government do that? One theory is that they were trying to hide a genetic experiment gone wrong. Perhaps the government created a **mutant** animal that escaped. That would explain why the Chupacabra is described as a combination of other animals, like lizards and kangaroos. Some even believe that the Chupacabra is a human-animal **hybrid**.

ALIEN PET?

If you think that theory is **far-fetched**, here's another one. Some conspiracy theorists believe that the Chupacabra is an alien, or an alien pet. The Arecibo Observatory in Puerto Rico is the world's largest radio-radar telescope that sends signals out into space. One hypothesis is that the telescope draws **UFOs** to the island and that Chupacabras were left behind on Earth.

▶ *Do you think that Earth is the only place in the universe with intelligent life? Perhaps other forms of intelligent life have been searching for us, the same way that we have been searching for them. Maybe they have already found us! Is it possible that they come for short visits to Earth, leaving their pets behind? Why might they do that?*

MONSTER HUNTERS

Reports of the Chupacabra killing livestock in Chile upset many people. The Government of Chile asked the National Guard to investigate what was behind the killings. The Government of Puerto Rico put the Civil Defense officials in charge of investigations. Many **amateur** hunters have also gone in search of the beast. Most have captured possums, coyotes, and other wild dogs, but none have brought home the elusive Chupacabra.

▶ Most monster hunters are serious investigators or even scientists. They carefully record every creature they capture while looking for the real Chupacabra.

Chupacabra Quest

In 2008, Ken Gerhard, a **cryptozoologist** who studies legendary creatures, went in search of Chupacabra for the History Channel's show *MonsterQuest*. Gerhard and Lee Hales, a wildlife expert from the US National Park Service, set out to look for evidence at Phylis Canion's ranch. The team set up motion-sensitive cameras on the property and used blood-soaked meat and a live chicken as bait. The two men waited, with night-vision goggles, for the Chupacabra to take the bait. In the morning, they found that the trap had worked. They had captured a scary beast... a possum! But the story doesn't end there. Two weeks later, Canion found another dead animal on her neighbor's property. It was a dog-type creature with long fangs and nails that looked like claws.

Did You Know?

While zoologists study animals and animal behavior, cryptozoologists explore—and search for—animals that have not yet been proven to exist. The word cryptozoology comes from Greek words meaning the "study of hidden animals." Cryptozoologists look for evidence that Bigfoot, Yeti, the Loch Ness Monster, or other legendary monsters (called cryptids) are real. The Chupacabra would be a prime catch.

Could It Be Real?

If the Chupacabra is real, what could it be? Perhaps it is a breed of wild dog that has never been seen before. It's not impossible. New species are found all the time. In 2013, glow-in-the dark cockroaches, skeleton shrimp, and a new type of dwarf lemur were discovered. Still, wild dogs generally eat the meat of their kills. They don't suck blood.

▲ When predators kill their prey, they eat as much meat as they can. Usually they leave only the bones for birds and smaller animals.

▶ The large flying fox, a type of megabat, lives in southeast Asia. One of the biggest types of bats, it can weigh 1.4–2.4 pounds (0.65–1.1 kg) and has a wingspan of almost 5 feet (1.5 m). Luckily, it does not suck blood. It eats only fruit, nectar, and flowers.

A GIANT BAT

Maybe Chupacabras are related to vampire bats, which live in Mexico and South America. These bats feed on fresh blood and hunt at night. They eat by biting a warm-blooded animal, making a small cut with their razor-sharp teeth, and licking up the blood with their tongues. Vampire bats usually feed on horses, cattle, and chickens, but are too small to kill their prey.

Scientists believe that in the Pleistocene era, a now **extinct** species of bat, known as a giant vampire bat, was 30 percent larger than the ones we see today. Is it possible that the animal is not really extinct? Species that were long thought to have been extinct have been found before.

> ▶ *Common vampire bats are small mammals and eat just 1 tablespoon (15 ml) of blood a day, not enough to kill the victim.*

DID YOU KNOW?

Evolution provides each animal with special skills or tools for survival. For vampire bats, one is a potion in their saliva that allows them to more easily feast on mammals. Bat saliva contains compounds that make their victim bleed longer. Think about what happens when you have a cut. Eventually it stops bleeding because the blood gets thick and clots. Bat saliva contains something called anticoagulants, which stops the blood from clotting. It also contains substances that stop the blood vessels near the wound from **constricting**.

Scientific View

Most scientists are **skeptical** about the idea that the Chupacabra is a monster, or even an unknown species. They prefer a more simple explanation—that Chupacabras are wild or domestic dogs. Witnesses like Phylis Canion describe Chupacabra skin as hairless, thick, and elephant-like. Mange, a disease caused by an eight-legged mite that digs under the skin, can affect dogs and leave their skin looking very similar to the description of Chupacabras. The skin becomes thicker, and their fur falls out.

▶ Coyotes, wild dogs, or foxes with severe cases of mange could be the real explanation for Chupacabras. These sick animals may attack livestock, which are easier prey than creatures hunted in the wild.

CHUPACABRA IN THE LAB

Scientific studies of Chupacabras have found no evidence that the livestock-killer is anything other than a dog with mange. Autopsies conducted on livestock supposedly killed by the beast show that they were not actually sucked dry of blood as witnesses believed. Scientists say that the holes left in the neck of the prey are consistent with puncture wounds from a dog's teeth. After all, that's what sharp canine teeth were designed for.

Researchers have also looked at **DNA** and hair evidence. Virtually all results point to a dog as the culprit. DNA taken from one specimen showed that it was a coyote, while samples from another belong to a domestic dog.

▶ The DNA taken from an unknown animal can be compared to the codes of known animals. This technology has been valuable to Chupacabra researchers.

CHUPACABRA COUSINS

Stories about blood-sucking monsters, like Chupacabra, are not new. Vampires are the most famous bloodsuckers of all. Vampires are said to survive by sucking and feeding on the blood of humans. Stories about vampires say that these "undead" creatures often visit loved ones and areas where they lived when they were alive.

Most cultures have stories about vampire-type creatures. However, the legends are most common in the Balkans and Eastern Europe.

▶ *Count Dracula is one of the most famous vampires. He is from Transylvania in Eastern Europe. In 1897, the horror novel* Dracula, *by Bram Stoker, introduced the legend to the world.*

JERSEY DEVIL AND MORE

The New Jersey Devils isn't just the name of an NHL team. It is also the name of a cryptid that apparently lives in Pine Barrens, New Jersey. The creature is said to look like a kangaroo with the head of a goat. It has wings, small arms with claws, and a blood-curdling scream.

The Sigbin of the Philippines is described as a goat-like beast that sucks the blood out of its victims. It has a long tail that it uses as a whip, as well as a horrible odor that can cause its prey to vomit. Like the Sigbin, the Chupacabra is also said to give off a nauseating odor. The monsters have something else in common—scientists do not believe that either are real.

▲ *Stories of the Sigbin say that the creature walks backwards with its head between its rear legs. It can also become invisible to others, such as humans.*

WHAT DO YOU THINK?

Could all of the witnesses who have claimed to see the Chupacabra be mistaken? Could they have actually just seen dogs with mange, as scientists believe? Eyewitnesses, including several ranchers in Texas, don't think so. They stress that they have seen mangy animals before and the Chupracabra sightings are different.

▶ Part of the difficulty with figuring out the mystery of the Chupacabra is that the descriptions of the creature vary so widely. The demon-like image seems to be fading away, while the dog-like monster is getting all of the fame now. Will the demon rear its ugly head again? Only time will tell.

UNSOLVED MYSTERY

There is no doubt that something killed the livestock in Puerto Rico and elsewhere. But if it wasn't for the Chupacabra tale, people may have assumed that the culprit was a coyote or wolf. It's hard to say how many of the Chupacabra reports are the result of people seeing something about the creature in the media or on the Internet.

Madelyne Tolentino had seen the movie *Species*, which may have affected her report of the creature. Newspapers picked up the Chupacabra story and spread it around. In 1996, a popular Spanish-language talk show from Miami, *Cristina*, dedicated an episode to the monster from Puerto Rico. Shortly after the show aired, the first Chupacabra sightings were reported in Miami. Was it a coincidence?

In the meantime, some sort of bloodthirsty beasts have been treating farms and ranches as their personal all-you-can-eat buffets. For now, the type of beast remains a mystery.

EYEWITNESS TALE

For years, residents of Turner, Maine, have reported incidents of dogs that have been **mauled** and of animals making strange cries in the night. In 2006, Michelle O'Donnell found a potential culprit, a dead animal off the side of the road, which she described as an "evil looking hybrid mutant." Her husband, Mike, described the fanged creature as a mix between a rodent and a dog. Unfortunately, the animal was never taken in for DNA testing.

GLOSSARY

amateur (A-muh-tur) A person who does something (such as a sport or hobby) for pleasure and not as a job.

autopsies (AW-top-seez) Operations performed on dead bodies to find out the cause of death.

carcass (KAHR-kus) The body of a dead animal.

conspiracy theorists (kun-SPEER-uh-see Thee-uh-rists) People who try to explain an event or situation as the result of a secret plan by usually powerful people or groups.

constricting (kun-STRIKT-ing) Making (something) narrower, smaller, or tighter.

cryptozoologist (KRIP-tow-zoh-ah-luh-jist) Someone who studies and searches for animals who may or may not exist.

culprit (KUL-prit) One accused or guilty of an offense.

DNA (DEE IN AY) A substance that carries genetic information in the cells of plants and animals.

extinct (ik-STINGKT) An animal that no longer exists.

far-fetched (FAR-FECHT) Not likely to happen or be true.

hoaxes (HOHKS-ez) Acts meant to trick people into believing or accepting as genuine things that are false and often preposterous.

hybrid (HY-brud) An animal or plant that is produced from two animals or plants of different kinds.

mauled (MAWLD) To attack and injure (someone) in a way that cuts or tears skin.

mutant (MYOO-tunt) A new organism resulting from a mutation of the original genetic make-up.

puncture (PUNGK-cher) To make a hole.

skeptical (SKEP-ti-kul) Having or expressing doubt about something (such as a claim or statement).

UFOs (YOO EF OHS) An object in the sky that has not been identified.

FOR MORE INFORMATION

FURTHER READING

Hayn, Carter. *Drawing Vampires*. Drawing Monsters Step-By-Step.
New York: Windmill Books, 2013.

Regan, Lisa. *Bloodsucking Beasts*. Monsters & Myths.
New York: Gareth Stevens, 2011.

Roberts, Steven. *Chupacabra!* Jr. Graphic Monster Stories.
New York: PowerKids Press, 2013.

WEBSITES

Due to the changing nature of Internet links, PowerKids Press has developed an online list of websites related to the subject of this book. This site is updated regularly. Please use this link to access the list:

www.powerkidslinks.com/mymo/chupa/

INDEX